Sources of Free Business Information

Sources of Free Business Information

Michael J Brooks

First published in Great Britain in 1986 by
Kogan Page Limited
120 Pentonville Road
London N1 9JN

British Library Cataloguing in Publication Data

Brooks, Michael
Sources of free business information.
1. Business — Bibliography
I. Title
016.338

ISBN 1-85091-113-4 Pbk

Printed and bound in Great Britain by
Billing & Sons Ltd, Worcester

Contents

Preface

The ever-increasing pace and complexity of modern business and commercial life have placed new pressures on businessmen and those who advise them. It is no longer feasible for even the best-informed businessman to have a detailed knowledge of all the legal, financial and economic factors which influence the course of his business; consequently he is more dependent than ever before on reliable and concise business information and advice.

The good news is that such information and advice are available. The even better news it that much of it is free and can be had just for the asking. This book offers a guide to some of the free information that is available and lists the names and addresses of those who produce it. Details are given of more than 400 books, leaflets and video tapes provided, or loaned, free of charge by some 90 commercial and professional organisations or government departments and agencies. Topics covered include taxation, sources of finance, government financial assistance, exporting and computers.

The items listed in this volume are probably only the tip of what could be an iceberg of considerable proportions. Readers who do not find exactly what they want here might be able to obtain the required material from other organisations similar to those listed. The larger firms of accountants and major banks are often the best places to try.

For whom is this book intended? Primarily for the smaller businessman who does not have an army of advisers and who needs to get the most out of those he has. However, many of the publications are likely to be of use and interest to students and librarians in universities and polytechnics, to consultants and to financial and business executives in larger organisations.

Readers will notice that no dates are given for any of the publications; this is because they are all updated regularly and when you ask for a booklet you will be sent the most recent edition.

To users of this guide I would like to say two things. First, please do not overdo your demands for publications. All the firms and agencies have indicated that they are happy to send copies of their publications to those who ask for them, but this could change if they are inundated with demands for 20 copies of everything they produce. Second, please send me details of any useful publications you yourselves discover so that I may include them in future editions.

And finally, a word to the providers. Keep up the good work and please let me know of any new or revised publications or of any publications that you think should have been included in this edition.

Michael J Brooks
January 1986

Chapter 1

Taxation

The system of direct and indirect taxation in the UK is complex and is constantly changing. The average businessman cannot expect to obtain more than a general understanding of the maze of detailed rules and regulations and will usually need to rely on his professional advisers to guide him through each particular labyrinth. As in many other business areas, however, the more informed businessman will be able to obtain a better service from his accountant in reducing the impact of the Inland Revenue's activities on his business.

Many of the booklets listed below are produced by firms of accountants, but the Inland Revenue also produces an excellent series of publications, and many of these are referred to in this chapter. These latter booklets usually set out the law and practice but cannot, of course, be relied on to provide many tax-saving hints!

General tax information

The Budget synopses, which are often available within 24 hours of the Budget speech, and other general tax background publications produced by the major accounting firms, are a useful source of information on the structure of, and latest developments in, tax matters.

Tax facts 1985-86. *Kidsons, 68pp.*
A brief but comprehensive description of income tax, National Insurance, corporation tax, capital gains tax, development land tax, capital transfer tax and VAT. Includes details of 1985-86 tax rates and allowances and useful sections on residence, benefits in kind and the Business Expansion Scheme (BES).

Doing business in the UK — taxation. *Deloitte Haskins and Sells, 43pp.*
Provides a broad outline of the UK tax system and describes the taxes on capital transactions and VAT. The appendices include current rates of tax and social security contributions.

The Finance Bill 1985 and **The Finance Act 1985.** *KMG Thomson McLintock, 48 and 58pp. respectively.*
Detailed and comprehensive descriptions of the Finance Bill and the subsequent Act as amended by Parliament. Each taxation change is fully explained and the background and implications are discussed. The Finance Act booklet contains a chapter on oil taxation.

Finance Act 1985. *Neville Russell, 36pp.*
A summary of the Finance Act which gives special attention to bond washing and coupon stripping.

Budget synopsis 1985. *Ernst and Whinney, 10pp.*
Budget synopsis 1985. *Hodgson Impey, 29pp.*
The Budget 1985. *Clark Whitehill, 25pp.*
The Budget 1985. *KMG Thomson McLintock, 32pp.*
Budget commentary 1985. *Binder Hamlyn, 55pp.*
Commentary on the Budget 1985 *Stoy Hayward, 37pp.*

These are examples of the kind of publication produced by all the major accounting firms. More comprehensive, more accurate and better laid out than the reports in even the best newspapers.

Tax facts and figures. *Coopers and Lybrand, 24pp.*
A genuinely pocket-sized guide to the main taxes, rates and reliefs. Amazingly wide coverage includes benefits in kind, residence rules and social security contributions and benefits.

Coming to the UK. *KMG Thomson McLintock, 42pp.*
Designed as a guide for foreign nationals coming to the UK to take up employment or for business activities, this booklet provides a complete introduction to the UK tax system, including social security and local authority rates. There is a useful chapter on tax planning.

Extra-statutory concessions. *Inland Revenue (IR 1), 46pp.*
Perhaps the nearest that the Inland Revenue gets to giving tax-saving advice! Separate chapters on concessions available to individuals and to companies. Covers all the main taxes.

Business taxation

Starting in business. *Inland Revenue (IR 28), 16pp.*
Provides an introduction to the taxation of business profits and covers the preparation of accounts, books and records, VAT and income tax. The appendices contain a simple worked example.

Corporation tax. *Inland Revenue (IR 18), 85pp.*
Explains the basis of corporation tax and contains a number of worked examples. A comprehensive and detailed booklet which includes a chapter on double taxation relief and a useful glossary.

Capital allowances on machinery and plant. *Inland Revenue (CA 1), 26pp.*
Outlines the main features of capital allowances (tax depreciation) and the type of expenditure that qualifies for relief. Contains worked examples.

Capital allowances on industrial buildings. *Inland Revenue (CA 2), 20pp.*
Describes the features of the scheme for granting tax depreciation on industrial buildings, explains how expenditure can qualify and provides worked examples.

Finance Bill 1985: impact on capital allowances. *Arthur Andersen, 4pp.*
Brief review of the changes in tax relief for capital expenditure and its implications.

Employers' guide to PAYE. *Inland Revenue (P 7), 67pp.*
Explains in detail the workings of the PAYE system and employers' responsibilities under it. Covers pay and tax records, coding, tax tables and procedures to cover (hopefully) every eventuality. A separate chapter is provided on expenses and benefits.

Tax and the privately-owned business. *Ernst and Whinney, 17pp.*
Covers briefly the taxation of sole traders, partnerships and companies and the effects of converting a business into a company. Further chapters outline the implications of introducing capital into a business and providing for retirement.

Tax: employed or self-employed? *Inland Revenue (IR 56), 7pp.*
Very brief but useful and authoritative discussion of self-employment and its taxation implications.

Benefits in kind. *Pannell Kerr Forster, 47pp.*
Describes how non-cash benefits are treated for tax and National Insurance purposes and provides some useful examples of 'tax-efficient' remuneration packages.

Employee benefits. *Kidsons, 11pp.*
Very brief but useful introduction to the subject of non-salary benefits and how they are taxed.

Key facts about employee benefits. *Sun Life of Canada, 25pp.*
Brief, pocket-sized guide which concentrates on pensions but includes several usefully summarised tables covering National Insurance contributions and benefits, retail price index and clearing-bank base rates.

Employee share schemes. *Ernst and Whinney, 44pp.*
Describes each of the various tax-efficient schemes available for providing incentives to employees: profit-sharing, share options and savings-related share schemes.

Shares for directors and employees. *Binder Hamlyn, 25pp.*
A guide to the legislation and practice covering share options and share-incentive schemes.

Notes on expenses payments and benefits for directors and certain employees. *Inland Revenue (IR 480), 53pp.*
Detailed and rather technical description of the tax treatment of expense payments. A useful chapter specifically lists non-taxable benefits.

Thinking of taking someone on? *Inland Revenue (IR 53), 9pp.*
Pamphlet on employers' tax responsibilities. Contains a useful 'child's guide' to a tax deduction worksheet.

Stock relief under the Finance Act 1981. *KMG Thomson McLintock, 202pp.*
Even though it has now been abolished, stock relief still affects many companies with open tax computations. This major publication covers all aspects of the topic and has a comprehensive index.

US corporate acquisitions: tax aspects for UK companies. *KMG Thomson McLintock, 40pp.*
The US accounting and tax regimes, which differ from those in Britain, offer both opportunities and dangers for UK companies taking over US companies. This guide covers the tax implications of such transactions and deals with the decision whether to purchase assets or shares, how to finance the acquisition and double taxation implications. Diagrams illustrate the use of a 'Swiss roundabout' and a Netherlands finance subsidiary.

Corporate year-end tax planning. *Arthur Andersen, 35pp.*
Guidance on the various possibilities for corporate tax planning and a brief summary of recent corporate tax changes. A particularly useful appendix summarises the time limits for certain reliefs and allowances; tax minimisation, it should be recognised, is usually a matter of careful planning.

Tax planning and the family company. *Peat Marwick Mitchell, 66pp.*
Tax planning for family companies involves consideration of both business and personal taxes and the way they interact with each other. This book covers remuneration, 'spreading income round the family', benefits in kind, pensions and the impact of capital transfer tax. Includes a list of other (free) Peat Marwick Mitchell publications.

The taxation of equipment leasing. *Peat Marwick Mitchell, 67pp.*
Recent tax changes have undermined much of the attractiveness of leasing, but it nevertheless remains a complex subject. Explains the tax aspects as they affect lessor and lessee.

To pay or not to pay: dividend considerations. *Dearden Farrow, 15pp.*
Discusses the relative advantages and disadvantages of dividends compared with the payment of remuneration by private companies. Recent changes in taxation and National Insurance rules have made the decision more evenly balanced than previously and the booklet advocates a flexible approach.

Revenue exchanges of information. *Arthur Andersen, 32pp.*
A very useful summary of the arrangements under which the Inland Revenue exchanges information with other national tax

authorities, particularly about the activities of multinationals. Very little published information is easily obtainable on this topic, which makes this booklet particularly welcome.

Energy finance tax aspects. *Ernst and Whinney, 20pp.* This publication originally appeared as an article in the book *Energy Finance* published in 1983 by Euromoney Publications. Explains the fiscal regime in the UK oil industry and its effect on the economics of both large and small oilfields. Provides a general description of the taxable capacity of the oil industry and its international aspects, together with comments on problem areas for oil-company finance managers and their bankers.

Personal taxation

General

Inland Revenue leaflets
Brief, but well-written leaflets cover the principal features of the UK personal tax system and how it works in practice. Each is pocket-sized and has between six and ten pages.

Income tax age allowance — more relief if you're over 65 (IR 4A)
Income tax: wife's earnings election (IR 13)
Income tax: personal allowances (IR 22)
Income tax and widows (IR 23)
Income tax and one-parent families (IR 29)
Income tax: separation and divorce (IR 30)
Income tax and married couples (IR 31)
Income tax: separate assessment (IR 32)
Income tax and school leavers (IR 33)
Income tax: Pay As You Earn (IR 34)
Income tax: SAYE share options (IR 38)
Income tax and the unemployed (IR 41)
Income tax: layoffs and short time (IR 42)
Income tax and strikes (IR 43)
What happens when someone dies (IR 45)
Your tax office: why it is where it is (IR 52)
Bank interest: paying tax (IR 55)
Capital gains tax: owner-occupied houses (CGT 4)
Capital gains tax and the small businessman (CGT 11)

Tax planning for the individual. *Ernst and Whinney, 24pp.* Covers tax-saving actions which can be taken by individuals before the end of the tax year (5 April). Includes income tax, capital gains tax and capital transfer tax. Published in January each year.

Residents and non-residents. *Inland Revenue (IR 20), 28pp.*
Describes the rules under which British expatriates and visitors to the UK become liable to UK taxes. Includes a short chapter on double taxation relief.

The taxation of foreign earnings and foreign pensions. *Inland Revenue (IR 25), 39pp.*
Goes into details of the rules applying to expatriates and recipients of foreign pensions. Technical but comprehensive.

Leaving the UK — a tax guide for UK residents. *KMG Thomson McLintock, 52pp.*
Describes the relevant rules and provides guidance for expatriates on the mitigation of tax liabilities. A useful checklist highlights the main points to be considered when working or living abroad.

Working in the UK. *Arthur Andersen, 81pp.*
A guide to the taxation of foreign nationals working in the UK, covering the principles and mechanics of the tax and the social security systems. Separate chapters cover immigration requirements and personal financial planning. The appendices include domicile and residence questionnaires and a reprint of a UK tax return.

Taxation of foreign nationals working in the UK. *Coopers and Lybrand, 29pp.*
Briefer than the Arthur Andersen booklet and based on five steps:

understanding basic principles
what to do before arrival in the UK
what to do on arrival in the UK
what to do at the end of the tax year
what to do when leaving the UK.

Taxation of holiday letting. *Dearden Farrow, 7pp.*
The 1984 Finance Act changed significantly the way holiday lettings are taxed. This brief guide covers the income tax and capital taxes aspects and shows that a holiday home may now be an economic proposition for a wide range of taxpayers.

Allied Dunbar guide to deeds of covenant. *Allied Dunbar Assurance, 35pp.*
Explains how this useful tax-saving mechanism works and provides a helpful flow chart which shows the steps in the

process. Includes a specimen deed of covenant (plus a Scottish version) and specimens of the relevant Inland Revenue forms.

Tax planning review. *Stoy Hayward, 47pp.*
Provides advice on how to reduce the impact of income tax and the capital taxes under the following headings:

avoiding a high taxable income
avoiding high taxable gains
avoiding a high chargeable estate.

The appendices include a list of shares which have been recognised by the Inland Revenue as having 'negligible value' and which can be charged as losses against capital gains tax.

Capital transfer tax

Much of the work of professional tax advisers relates to capital transfer tax, for which detailed planning may be required over many years. A reasonable understanding of the basic principles of this tax will enable the taxpayer to obtain the maximum benefit from his advisers. Information is also available on the Inheritance Tax which will replace CTT.

Capital transfer tax. *Inland Revenue (CTT 1), 125pp.*
A thorough, detailed, somewhat technical publication which is perhaps more suited to the professional adviser than the average taxpayer. Useful for students.

Allied Dunbar guide to capital transfer tax. *Allied Dunbar, 79pp.*
Provides a comprehensive description of the tax and stresses the point that planning can reduce its impact. Excludes some of the more esoteric aspects and, not surprisingly, discusses in some detail the role of life assurance in CTT mitigation. The appendices are particularly useful, covering additional points for director-shareholders of private companies and special opportunities for farmers.

Capital transfer tax — some constructive suggestions. *Pannell Kerr Forster, 19pp.*
A short but well-structured guide to the basics of CTT and how its effect can be reduced. Useful worked examples.

Give now save later and **Use your discretion.** *Dearden Farrow, 9 and 8pp. respectively.*
Two booklets covering the use of lifetime exemptions and discretionary trusts to reduce the final CTT bill. The basics are well explained.

Taxation of UK trusts. *Hodgson Impey, 28pp.*
Covers not only capital transfer tax but also income tax, capital gains tax, development land tax and stamp duty. Good, clear worked examples.

Passing money to your children. *Peat Marwick Mitchell, 96pp.*
Outlines the CTT rules on passing money to children and explains the reliefs and exemptions which enable those who plan ahead to maximise the amount that goes to the family. Aspects discussed include covenants, investments, houses and land, businesses, farms, woodlands, charities and wills.

Value added tax

The booklets produced by the Department of Customs and Excise, which administers VAT, are well-written and comprehensive.

Should you be registered for VAT? 12pp.
Filling in your VAT return. 6pp. plus specimen return
The ins and outs of VAT. 11pp.
Visits by VAT officers. 8pp.
Keeping records and accounts. 12pp. plus specimen VAT invoice.

The department also produces a wide range of more detailed publications. A full list can be obtained from the address given in Chapter 11.

Guide to saving VAT. *Deloitte Haskins and Sells, 63pp.*
VAT is often considered to be an unavoidable burden, but this booklet highlights a number of ways in which businesses can make savings, either by reducing the amount of VAT they have to bear as an expense or by improving their cash flow. Each aspect is considered in a separate section and a planning summary is provided at the end of the booklet.

Proposals for the enforcement of VAT. *Arthur Andersen, 4pp.*
Brief description of the provisions of the 1985 Act for the more rigorous enforcement of VAT and the civil and criminal sanctions to be applied.

Specialised areas

Taxation of Lloyd's members. *Neville Russell, 59pp.*
Provides an outline of the Lloyd's insurance market and, in particular, the taxation implications of underwriting membership. The introduction includes an interesting account of the history of Lloyd's, its membership requirements and obligations and how income arises and is accounted for. Tax aspects covered include US and Canadian as well as UK tax. The appendices include a glossary of terms and sample US tax returns.

The Business Expansion Scheme. *Inland Revenue (IR 51), 8pp.*
Sets out the objectives and workings of the BES in non-technical language.

Business Expansion Scheme. *Hodgson Impey, 20pp.*
Well set-out introduction to the scheme which includes a short section on tax planning considerations and pitfalls, plus worked examples.

Taxation for farmers Part I — capital transfer tax and **Taxation for farmers Part II — taxation of income.** *Hodgson Impey, 16 and 34pp. respectively.*
Companion volumes which together cover all the principal tax provisions applicable specifically to agriculture. Includes the formation of farming companies and the taxation of woodlands. The relevant tax cases are quoted.

Farmers' guide to PAYE. *Inland Revenue (P 5), 38pp.*
Starting with a general introduction to PAYE, covers the application of the system to unincorporated farming employers.

Allied Dunbar guide to capital taxes and agricultural property. *Allied Dunbar, 23pp.*
Explains how to mitigate capital transfer tax, outlines the reliefs available and discusses the incidental capital gains tax implications. Includes a summary of CTT and CGT planning

considerations for farmers and landowners and a warning about the impact of stamp duty.

Charities and charitable gifts — UK tax guide. *Binder Hamlyn, 17pp.*
Covers both the taxation and the exemption from taxation of charities and tax-efficient contributions to charities by businesses and individuals. Contains specimen deeds of covenant of both 'net' and 'gross' varieties.

Double taxation relief. *Inland Revenue (IR 6), 34pp.*
Explains the principles of double taxation relief and the types of double taxation agreement. Provides plenty of worked examples and a list of double taxation agreements in force.

Construction industry tax deduction scheme *(IR 14/15)* and **Conditions for getting a sub-contractor's tax certificate.** *(IR 40), Inland Revenue, 65 and 5pp. respectively.*
The particular circumstances of a contractor-sub-contractor relationship in the construction industry have given rise to a body of special arrangements which are outlined in these two publications. IR 14/15 explains the scheme in detail and describes the procedures involved; it includes the information contained in IR 40. The appendices contain useful guidance on checking sub-contractors' tax certificates; the point is made that failure to do this properly can lead to the payment of the tax by the contractor.

Taxation and sport. *Arthur Andersen, 27pp.*
Description of the taxes which affect sports clubs, associations, leagues and governing bodies. The guide also highlights the taxes which sports people may suffer on cash payments and benefits in kind. A separate section advises on the importance of tax aspects in fund raising and the financing of capital projects.

Employers' National Insurance contributions. *Hodgson Impey, 13pp. (Technical Bulletin)*
National Insurance contributions by employers, while not a tax in the technical sense, represent a considerable burden on businesses. This 'Technical Bulletin' outlines the basis of the charge and analyses various methods by which the burden can be reduced.

Chapter 2

Sources of Business Finance

In the recent past the financing of industry and commerce has become much more complex. The expansion and diversification of the financial markets and increased competition between the providers and the seekers of finance have contributed to this situation. It is, therefore, more important than ever that businessmen acquire a level of familiarity with the new environment which will enable them to compete effectively in the financial as well as the commercial marketplace.

Borrowing from banks

Finance for industry and commerce. *Forward Trust Group, 8pp.*
A brief summary of the principal types of finance available from banks.

Finance for business. *Midland Bank, 11pp.*
Another brief guide to the main types of finance available.

Borrowing from your bank. *Bank of Scotland, 9pp.*
One of the 'Guides for businessmen' series of booklets, it provides guidance on how to present a case to a bank and explains how the bank manager will evaluate the proposal put to him.

How to present a financial case to a bank. *Ernst and Whinney, 12pp.*
Particularly directed towards the owners of small or newly established businesses who may require external finance for the first time. Includes: presenting a financial case, preparing trading and cash flow projections and a description of the types of finance available and likely sources.

Borrowing money for capital projects. *Investors in Industry, 12pp.*
Designed for small or medium-sized firms, this booklet covers the types of borrowing available and contains a useful explanation of financial gearing and risk. Numerical examples are provided and a question-and-answer chapter.

The British banking system. *National Westminster Bank, 24pp.*
Provides the businessman (and business student) with an excellent summary of the banking system in Britain, its composition and regulation. Includes a short glossary of banking terms.

Acceptance credits. *Barclays Merchant Bank, 11pp.*
Basis loans. *Barclays Merchant Bank, 6pp.*
Development capital. *Barclays Merchant Bank, 7pp.*
Replacement capital. *Barclays Merchant Bank, 6pp.*

This series of leaflets describes several different types of short- and longer-term finance which are available to the smaller company and with which it may not be familiar. Useful background for the businessman who needs something more than a straightforward loan.

International Banking. *Price Waterhouse, 91pp.*
Provides a detailed and comprehensive review of the money markets operating in the City of London and the regulatory framework that applies to the banking sector. Useful for finance directors and students of business studies and economics.

Raising venture capital

Sources of venture capital in the UK. *Stoy Hayward, 50pp.*
Describes the main features of the venture capital market in the UK, including the taxation implications and the Business Expansion Scheme. The second half of the book lists 77 providers of venture finance and describes the type, size and duration of the investment each undertakes.

Raising venture capital. *Deloitte Haskins and Sells, 122pp.*
Subtitled 'An entrepreneur's guidebook', this publication is aimed particularly at the high-technology sector. It emphasises

the need to draw up detailed business plans before approaching the providers of venture finance. Chapters cover establishing the business, the format of the plan and the information it should contain, as well as advice on the selection of, and negotiations with, venture capital firms. A particularly useful ten-page glossary is provided.

Corporate venturing. *Arthur Andersen, 12pp.*
Refers to the provision of venture capital by large corporations, not only for direct financial return, but also as an aid to product diversification and technological advance. The booklet describes some of the factors which have given rise to this activity, highlights the opportunities available and describes the critical success factors in this form of investment.

Business plans and financing proposals. *Arthur Andersen/British Venture Capital Association. 32pp.*
Emphasises the fact that the development of a business plan is the critical stage in the process of finding a suitable source of venture capital. Part I describes how the plan is put together and part II provides a pro-forma outline plan and comments on its probable contents.

Raising equity capital

General

Going public: a guide to Stock Exchange listings and the Unlisted Securities Market. *Barclays Merchant Bank, 19pp.*
An introductory booklet which outlines the legal and business implications of raising equity capital on the stock market. Includes a useful section on the alternatives to going public.

Should you go public? *Robson Rhodes, 12pp.*
Another introductory publication covering much the same ground as the Barclays booklet.

Going public in the UK. *Samuel Montagu, 16pp.*
A somewhat more detailed publication which includes a useful glossary of terms.

Community capital markets: Part I — conditions for listing and **Community capital markets: Part II — half-yearly reporting requirements.** *Deloitte Haskins and Sells, both 29pp.*
These two booklets outline the provisions of the European Community directive on the admission of securities to listing and the subsequent reporting requirements. These provisions are now part of the London Stock Exchange requirements and the booklets explain how implementation will affect the remaining countries of the EEC.

The Unlisted Securities Market

The Unlisted Securities Market — a general guide. *Hacker Young, 8pp.*
A brief introduction to the USM which includes a reprint of the general undertaking that companies quoted on the Unlisted Securities Market are required to make.

The Unlisted Securities Market. *KMG Thomson McLintock, 55pp.*
Comprehensive coverage of the subject, including sections on using professional advisers (not only accountants) and the cost of doing so, upgrading from a USM quote to a full Stock Exchange listing and the taxation implications.

Guide to the Unlisted Securities Market. *Arthur Andersen, 47pp.*
Special attention is given to the accounting and reporting requirements and to the mechanics of entry to the USM. The appendices are particularly interesting; they include analyses of USM companies by year and method of entry and by price/earnings ratios, also an analysis of companies which have left the USM, by graduating to a full listing, because they were taken over or went into liquidation.

A guide to the Unlisted Securities Market. *Ernst and Whinney, 30pp.*
A comprehensive guide, which underlines the importance of planning in making a successful entry to the USM.

The Unlisted Securities Market. *Arthur Young, 37pp.*
Well-structured booklet which shows the steps to be taken in order to achieve entry to the market. A useful chapter discusses

events after flotation. A glossary of terms is provided.

The USM. *Deloitte Haskins and Sells, video tape, 20 minutes.*
Well-presented video which describes the background to the formation of the USM and includes interviews with owner-directors of successful USM launches. Available on free loan.

Stock Exchange listing

Obtaining a Stock Exchange quotation. *Stoy Hayward, 21pp.*
Basic information on the possibility, desirability and mechanics of obtaining a full quotation on the Stock Exchange. The appendices include a guide to the costs.

Going public in the UK. *Ernst and Whinney, 14pp.*
Concentrates on the accountant's report and the preparation of the prospectus. Two particularly useful features are a diagram of the timetable to be followed before and after flotation and a four-page glossary which explains and defines the main technical financial terms used.

Prospectuses and circulars of listed companies: checklist of contents. *Arthur Young, 121pp.*
One of Arthur Young's 'Focus on capital markets' series. A substantial publication which covers Stock Exchange requirements in respect of:

> new listings
> share issues by an existing listed company
> debt issues by an existing listed company
> significant acquisitions and disposals
> transactions involving directors or substantial shareholders.

The book is set out in checklist form which makes it particularly easy to use.

The new Yellow Book. *KMG Thomson McLintock, 21pp.*
The Yellow Book sets out the official requirements of the Stock Exchange for the listing of shares and loan capital. This booklet describes and explains the contents of the new edition, which came into effect on 1 January 1985, and the changes in its status and its requirements.

Foreign companies — a guide to a UK listing. *Arthur Young, 43pp.*
Another of the 'Focus on capital markets' series, this book is written for foreign public companies considering a UK quotation. It explains the principal features of the London Stock Market and the possible advantages of a quotation and covers the mechanics of obtaining a listing.

A London listing — a guide to secondary quotations for overseas companies. *Samuel Montagu, 15pp.*
Similar to the Arthur Young publication but briefer, this booklet contains a useful timetable, checklists and a glossary.

Public offerings in the United States and **Deciding to go public in the United States.** *Ernst and Whinney, 16 and 62pp. respectively.*
The first publication outlines the regulatory framework under which public offerings of securities are made in the USA and describes briefly the disclosure requirements. The second discusses in more detail the technical requirements and restrictions relevant to a public offering of securities in the USA and the many practical business considerations that have to be taken into account. Both contain good glossaries.

Chapter 3

Official Grants and Incentives

Enormous amounts of EEC, UK government and local government financial aid are available to those who qualify, and — more importantly — know that it is available. The publications listed below may provide a starting point for the businessman who believes that he could be eligible for this aid. In addition, the Department of Trade and Industry is a source of much useful information and advice.

Official sources of finance and aid for industry in the UK. *National Westminster Bank, 66pp.*
This book, normally sold for £5.50, is available free of charge to certain non-profit making bodies, such as chambers of commerce and business advisory units. It is comprehensive and detailed and provides information on regional aid and nationally available aid for each industry sector. There are separate chapters on aid for energy conservation projects, employment and training, aid for exporters and aid from the various European Community agencies. The appendices include a full list of the relevant addresses and telephone numbers. Worth the cover price if you do not qualify for a free copy.

Invest in Britain. *Invest in Britain Bureau, pack of 19 leaflets.*
Intended primarily for companies considering setting up or expanding an operation in the UK, the leaflets cover, *inter alia*, the following topics:

Finance from European sources
UK financial incentives
National selective assistance
Regional investment incentives
Local assistance to industry.

Greater Manchester Economic Development Corporation information pack. *GMEDC, pack of 10 booklets.*
This is just one example (and a very professionally produced one) of the information on regional and local incentives

available from sponsoring development agencies. The pack is comprehensive and includes details of subsidised seminars and the full range of national, regional, local, educational and taxation incentives on offer to firms in the Greater Manchester area.

Investing in Scotland. *Royal Bank of Scotland, 22pp.*
There are chapters describing financial incentives, including tax and service industry assistance, available to businesses investing in Scotland.

Summary of financial incentives for businesses in Scotland. *Royal Bank of Scotland, 29pp.*
A concise, comprehensive leaflet containing sections on support for innovation and special agencies and schemes.

Government help for your business. *Binder Hamlyn, 76pp.*
A thorough description of the assistance available in the UK. Chapters on advisory assistance schemes, research and development, exporting and assistance for tourism and recreation projects.

Public money for business projects. *Kidsons, 24pp.*
A brief guide to regional and other assistance, including energy efficiency grants and support for innovation.

Finance for business Part 1 — government assistance. *KMG Thomson McLintock, 96pp.*
Written with the support of the Department of Trade and Industry this guide covers the whole range of regional and national assistance. It is set out logically, by locality and by topic. A separate section outlines EEC assistance and the appendices include a useful index of abbreviations and a list of contact addresses and telephone numbers.

Government and EEC grants and assistance to businesses in the UK. *Hacker Young, 99pp.*
Covers much the same ground as the Thomson McLintock publication, but includes a whole section on small firms. Appendix 1 provides a guide to the assistance available to businesses of different size and type cross-referenced to the main body of the book.

Bank of Scotland Government Assistance Information Services (GAINS) 1 industry and tourism and **2 agriculture, forestry and fishing.** *Bank of Scotland, 35 and 4pp. respectively.*
Separate chapters on each of the main sources of EEC and UK government aid and a useful list of further sources of information and advice.

Grant-aided consultancy. *Neville Russell, 3pp.*
Explains how government assistance can be made available for a variety of business consultancy services.

Official sources of financial and other assistance for UK industry. *Armitage and Norton, 127pp.*
A comprehensive compendium of the various types of assistance available through central and local government. Separate chapters cover:

regional assistance
national investment assistance
transport incentives
research, development and innovation
employment and training
energy-related assistance
exports
special assistance to small firms
agriculture and forestry
tourism and leisure
European Community assistance.

Each entry describes the type and level of assistance granted and explains any restrictions that apply. A full set of addresses and telephone numbers is provided.

Financial incentives and assistance for industry. *Arthur Young, 156pp.*
Another excellent publication, containing separate chapters on:

investment support
support for innovation
business and technical advice
exports
employment and training
local initiatives to help business

agriculture, natural resources, energy and transport.

Appendices cover regional assistance and include a section on financial assistance, taxation and maps.

Tourism and leisure: investing in the future. *English Tourist Board, 16pp.*
Describes the investment opportunities in the tourism and leisure industries in England and explains how the ETB can provide financial and advisory assistance with projects.

Chapter 4

Exporting and Doing Business Overseas

A great deal of information is available to businesses that wish to develop export markets or do business overseas. Much of this information is provided by the international banks and the major firms of accountants and it can be of considerable value in identifying possible overseas markets and developing strategies for exploiting international business opportunities.

Exporting

Help for exporters. *British Overseas Trade Board, 47pp.*
Summarises the services provided to exporters by the BOTB. Topics covered include getting into the market, specialist advice and help with major projects. There is an application form to be filled in by those wishing to be put on the BOTB free mailing list and receive information about special initiatives, new schemes and later editions of the booklet.
NB The BOTB annual report contains useful background information about export projects and particular opportunities as well as providing a review of the year's activities.

UK exporters' financial procedures. *British Overseas Trade Board, 15pp.*
Summarises the results of a survey carried out for the BOTB on export financing practice in the UK. The results show a wide variety of practice and divergent attitudes towards risk-taking. The fact that some of the risk-taking may have been inadvertent underlines the need for specialist, impartial advice.

ECGD services. *Exports Credits Guarantee Department, 53pp.*
A detailed description of export finance risks and of how the services of the ECGD can be used to reduce them. A 15-minute video tape is also available on free loan.

Entering an export market. *Midland Bank International, 19pp.*
Outlines the steps that need to be taken in order to develop a particular export market. Chapters cover researching the market, visiting the market and setting up an overseas operation. A useful list of contacts is provided.

Services for exporters. *Midland Bank, 44pp.*
A comprehensive description of export marketing, documentation, payment methods and finance and credit insurance. Includes a reference guide, not only to further Midland Bank publications, but also to a number of other free publications. Unusually for a book this size, an index is provided.

Getting into ECGD. *Export Credits Guarantee Department, 16pp.*
Sizing up the buyer risk. *Export Credits Guarantee Department, 11pp.*
Using the credit limit service. *Export Credits Guarantee Department, 7pp.*
Cutting your losses. *Export Credits Guarantee Department, 12pp.*
These short booklets cover individual aspects of the services provided by ECGD and include information on how to assess the creditworthiness of overseas buyers and how to minimise potential losses on overseas sales.

What you need to make export a safer world. *Trade Indemnity, folder containing 38 sheets.*
Description of the various credit insurance facilities and the risks they are intended to cover; specimen policy included. Useful background information whether or not you take a policy with this company.

Tradebrief. *Midland Bank, 4-page monthly news sheet.*
Highlights business opportunities and economic and fiscal developments overseas. The Bank provides a telephone and telex follow-up service for readers who are interested in particular items.

Guide to exporting and importing. *National Westminster Bank, 38pp.*
A guide to the terminology and procedures of international

trade. Advice and information are given on finding customers and suppliers, financing, trade regulations and the despatch and receipt of goods. The section on procedures provides a brief description of the terms of overseas contracts, methods of payment and documentation. Helpful suggestions are made regarding training and further reading.

Export insurance and finance. *National Westminster Bank, 25pp.*
Describes the types of policies available from the ECGD and suggests some non-insurance alternatives. The financing section explains the range of short- and long-term facilities available and illustrates their operation by means of clear and colourful diagrams.

Documentary credits. *National Westminster Bank, 34pp.*
Documentary credits are now an established feature of international trade and this booklet describes how they work. The text is complemented by particularly clear diagrams and sample documents. A glossary of terms and abbreviations is included.

The ten-page companion checklist provides a step-by-step guide through the various procedures and covers practically every conceivable problem area concerning the letter of credit itself and the related insurance, commercial and freight documentation. Very useful.

Foreign bonds and guarantees. *National Westminster Bank, 24pp.*
Describes the bonds and guarantees required by overseas customers to support contractual obligations entered into by UK exporters, to ensure that the terms of the order will be complied with. The different types of bonds and guarantees are described and illustrated and advice is given on the wording to be used. The appendix provides a full set of specimens of the model forms.

Business information on individual countries

Most large banking groups and international firms of accountants produce a wealth of information on countries within their area of interest. The selection listed below is only the tip of the iceberg. The best approach will often be to identify the major banks serving the country or area you are interested in and to contact them directly. Most international banks have offices in London and a full list is provided in *Crawfords Directory of City Connections* (Economist Publications) which, unfortunately, is far from free at £87.50!

Business profile series. *Hongkong and Shanghai Banking Corporation/British Bank of the Middle East.*
An excellent series of booklets of up to 60 pages providing a comprehensive and detailed review of the country in question. Most follow the same pattern, with a general introduction, a review of the economy, a series of statistics and chapters on business information and information for visitors and residents. The appendices include the addresses of government departments, trade organisations and embassies. This series currently covers the following countries:

Bahrain
Brunei
Chile
China
Cyprus
Djibouti
Egypt
Hong Kong
India
Indonesia
Japan
Jordan
Korea
Macao
Malaysia
Mauritius
Oman
Pakistan
Papua New Guinea
Philippines
Qatar
Saudi Arabia
Singapore
Solomon Islands
Sri Lanka
Taiwan
Thailand
United Arab Emirates
Vanuatu
Yemen Arab Republic

Business information series. *Standard Chartered Bank.*
These booklets are briefer than the Hongkong and Shanghai series, but are also designed to provide an overview of each country and its business environment. The same pattern is adopted for each booklet, ie background information, establishing a business in the country, trading with the country, banking and a selection of useful addresses. Countries covered are:

Bahrain	Oman
Bangladesh	Pakistan
Botswana	Qatar
China	Singapore
Hong Kong	Thailand
India	United Arab Emirates
Korea	Zambia
Malaysia	Zimbabwe
Nigeria	

NB The above two series would be of considerable use to students and senior school children.

Establishing a business in Australia. *Westpac Banking Corporation, 73pp.*
Detailed information on a wide range of topics relevant to establishing a business in Australia. Subjects covered are the general business background, government policy on investment by foreigners, types of business organisation, taxation, government and industry, basic services, raw materials and information for executives moving to Australia.

150,000 business opportunities in Australia. *Westpac International Business Advisory Service (WIBAS), Westpac Banking Corporation.*
This is a free, computerised trade and investment service from Westpac providing information for potential investors and international marketers in Australia.

Australia: guidelines for foreign investment. *ANZ Banking Corporation, 7pp.*
Describes the Australian government's policy towards investment by foreigners and how this policy is administered, explaining how proposed investments are screened and what criteria are used in their evaluation. A separate section outlines exchange control arrangements.

Business in Australia. *ANZ Banking Corporation, 13pp.*
A brief guide designed for the business migrant or investor.

The Channel Islands: a business and tax profile. *Pannell Kerr Forster, 28pp.*
A general introduction to the business and fiscal environment in

the Channel Islands including the regulations regarding immigration. There is a brief summary of the double taxation arrangements between the UK and the Channel Islands in an appendix.

Jersey — the international financial centre. *Dearden Farrow, 14pp.*
This pocket guide outlines the attractions of Jersey as a business centre and describes briefly the legal and taxation environment in which businesses operate on the island.

The Channel Islands: financial benefits and the legal background. *Deloitte Haskins and Sells, 39pp.*
Designed primarily as a guide to the business advantages of the Channel Islands, this booklet also deals with subjects of interest to those who are considering moving to the Channel Islands for retirement. An introductory chapter outlines the history, constitution and status of the islands and later sections cover company law, taxation and the requirements for establishing residence and setting up a business.

Trading in Guernsey and **Trading in the Isle of Man.** *Clark Whitehill, 10 and 15pp. respectively.*
These companion booklets cover the economies, taxation and company law in the respective islands and offer advice on trading and information on employment conditions.

Executive guide to the countries of ASEAN. *Citibank, 90pp.*
Covering Indonesia, Malaysia, Philippines, Singapore and Thailand, this book provides information on each country under the following headings:

background information
foreign investment opportunities
foreign investment regulations
forms of business enterprise
doing business
labour
taxation
banking and finance
communications
visiting
living there.

Pocket guides. *Arthur Andersen.*
This series of leaflets (each approximately 10pp.) provides a selection of key information on the principal European countries: the economy, company law, taxation and immigration.

Taxation in . . . and **Investment in . . .** *Peat Marwick Mitchell.*
Two series of booklets (of up to 100pp. each) covering the main developed and developing countries of the world (list available on request). The 'Investment in' series provides a brief survey of the economy of each country, its company law, direct and indirect taxation, social security, banking and financial systems and government incentives and controls. The accounting practice is also outlined where this differs from UK practice.

The 'Taxation in' series provides a more detailed analysis of the various taxes, their principles and how they are administered and outlines the relevant double taxation agreements.

Doing business in the European Community. *Touche Ross, 296pp.*
This hard-back book deals with all the more important aspects of business life in the European Community. Its four main sections cover:

community institutions and the decision-making process
exporting, investing, influencing and monitoring
internal community policies which concern business
external community policies which concern business.

Particularly useful features are a list of contact addresses and telephone numbers, a list of suggested further reading and a short glossary of terms and abbreviations.

Italian exports. *Banco di Roma, 38pp.*
Provides details of insurance, financing and special concessions available to Italian exporters.

Company income tax in Italy. *Banco di Roma, 92pp.*
Written especially for companies considering setting up an operation in Italy, this book outlines Italian company law and describes the principles and mechanics of company taxation.

General international information

World holiday and time guide. *Morgan Guaranty Trust Co, 125pp.*
A useful and fascinating little book which gives details of the public holidays and time zones of more than 200 countries around the world. The holiday information is analysed by country and by date.

Prices and earnings around the globe. *Union Bank of Switzerland, 42pp.*
Compares the cost of living in 49 cities around the world. The appendices show the earnings and working hours in each of the cities of 12 occupational groups from bus drivers to departmental managers.

Foreign exchange information: a worldwide summary. *Price Waterhouse, 163pp.*
Provides details of the more important aspects of foreign currency transactions in 96 countries: the currency unit, its linkage (if any) to other currencies and restrictions on cash movements and account transfers into and out of the country.

International insolvency. *KMG Thomson McLintock, 167pp.*
Summarises the insolvency law and practice in 32 countries. Each section explains the legislative authority regulating insolvency and the main features of receiverships and liquidations and the rights of creditors.

Foreign exchange. *National Westminster Bank, 14pp.*
Summarises the foreign exchange aspects of international trading and explains the principal mechanisms of the foreign exchange market. Forward contracts and the relationship between forward rates and spot rates are discussed and an explanation is given of the use of currency finance and how foreign exchange exposure can be reduced by factoring and hedging.

A guide to European exchange controls. *Arthur Andersen, 107pp.*
A useful booklet providing basic information about exchange controls in Austria, Belgium, Denmark, Finland, France, West

Germany, Greece, Ireland, Italy, Luxembourg, the Netherlands, Norway, Portugal, Spain, Sweden, Switzerland, Turkey and the UK.

Exploring countertrade opportunities. *Business International, 56pp.*
Countertrade, or barter as it used to be called, is now big business, particularly for companies that trade with the Third World. This publication describes the principal features of this activity and its advantages and disadvantages. The attitudes of the major trading nations to countertrade are reviewed and the development of a countertrade strategy is outlined. The final section contains practical advice on negotiating countertrade contracts.

Chapter 5

General Economic and Business Information

Economic information

The major UK and international banks produce economic surveys which are both authoritative and independent. These banks will usually issue them free of charge to anyone who requests them, and the initial approach should be made to the economics department at the head office of the bank in question at the address shown in Chapter 11. These publications provide essential background for businessmen and their advisers and are also very useful for students of business and economics who need to know what is happening in the economy.

The **Quarterly Economic Reviews** produced by the major UK clearing banks, ie Barclays, Lloyds, Midland, National Westminster, Standard Chartered, Bank of Scotland and the Royal Bank of Scotland contain articles on general economic and business topics written by distinguished academics, bankers and industrialists. **The Standard Chartered Review** is somewhat different, providing a monthly update on economic developments in the principal countries of Africa, the Middle East and Asia.

Monthly summary of business conditions in the UK. *Royal Bank of Scotland.*
This pocket-sized leaflet of approximately 7pp. provides graphs, statistics and a short commentary on seven topics: production and employment, overseas transactions, prices and wages, industrial investment, banking, short-term interest rates and Stock Exchange indices.

Britain: the economy in figures. *Lloyds Bank, 4pp.*
An annual, pocket-sized leaflet which contains statistics on national income, production, manpower and incomes, prices, overseas trade, government and commercial finance and

indicators of the standard of living and consumer expenditure.

Britain: an economic profile. *Lloyds Bank, 24pp.*
A companion leaflet to the one described above, this publication provides background and commentary to supplement the bare statistics.

Economic and financial outlook. *National Westminster Bank.*
Published quarterly and comprising 15-20pp. this bulletin summarises world economic news and trends and contains a comprehensive set of statistical information.

Economic report: Northern Ireland and **Economic report: Republic of Ireland.** *Bank of Ireland, 5pp. each.*
These parallel publications are produced quarterly and summarise economic conditions and trends.

International financial outlook. *Lloyds Bank, 4pp.*
A monthly commentary on recent trends in and the outlook for the major world trading currencies.

World financial markets. *Morgan Guaranty Trust Co, quarterly, approx 12pp.*
Commentary on monetary trends and issues particularly in the USA and Europe. The statistical appendix covers a wide range of information from exchange rates to interest rates and bond yields.

Business forecast. *Charterhouse Japhet, 12pp.*
Summarises current economic conditions in the UK and the USA and forecasts developments in such areas as money supply, prices and output. A comparison of economic forecasts made by other commentators (mainly banks) of growth in output, inflation, the balance of payments and unemployment is provided.

Annual sterling review. *Samuel Montagu, 50-60pp.*
A thorough review of UK financial and economic activity, covering the UK economy, sterling loans and acceptances, the equity market, the bulldog and Eurosterling bond markets, corporate finance activity and money market statistics.

Quarterly international investment review. *Kleinwort Benson, 20pp.*
An assessment of the economic and financial condition of the major economies of North America, Europe and the Far East, covering the state of the economy, interest rates and stock market trends.

Economic progress report. *HM Treasury, 8pp.*
This monthly booklet covers all aspects of the UK economy, noting trends and developments in the financial markets, monetary measures, employment, earnings and labour costs, public sector finance, output and the balance of payments. Graphs show the past five years' trends in the money supply, prices, output, unemployment, the balance of payments and exchange rates.

Economic perspective. *Schroders, 4pp.*
A brief, quarterly review of the short-term economic outlook in the UK and a report on the capital markets and economic indicators.

International perspective. *Schroders, 4pp.*
Complementary to the above publication, this quarterly leaflet puts the UK's economic performance and prospects into an international context.

Economic newsletter. *Banque Nationale de Paris, 8pp.*
This bimonthly booklet provides an overview of the French economy and contains articles on the economies of France's main trading partners.

Business indicators. *ANZ Banking Group, approx 6pp.*
Provides an update on the Australian economy. A series of graphs show five-year trends in employment, prices, retail sales, vehicle registrations, housing starts, investment, share indices, money supply, bank deposits and interest and exchange rates.

Monthly survey. *Taiyo Kobe Bank, 4pp.*
Commentaries on economic and industrial trends in Japan.

Economic bulletin. *Lloyds Bank, 4pp.*
This monthly bulletin covers selected economic topics and includes a useful commentary on recent changes in the major economic indicators.

Business information

Kidsons digest. *Kidsons, 12pp.*
A useful monthly review of financial and business news covering taxation, computer topics, company law, investments and personal finance.

Briefing. *Binder Hamlyn, 12pp.*
Similar in structure and content to the Kidsons publication, this monthly booklet includes a regular feature on information technology and updates the list of Binder Hamlyn free publications on business and taxation topics.

Financial account. *Robson Rhodes, 8pp.*
More newsy than the above two publications, this monthly leaflet contains items on taxation, accounting, company law and current business and political issues.

Business review. *Arthur Young, 24pp.*
A quarterly publication more substantial than the above three, containing a number of articles on business and management topics. The spring edition includes a budget commentary. Additions to the firm's list of free publications are described.

Trading in the United Kingdom. *Clark Whitehill, 36pp.*
Designed principally for overseas enterprises considering setting up business in the UK, this booklet provides a useful summary of the economic, political and tax environment in the UK. Topics covered include the regulatory background, forms of business organisation and the taxation of companies and individuals.

Doing business in the UK: types of business organisation. *Deloitte Haskins and Sells, 20pp.*
Several types of business organisation can be used as vehicles for trading in the UK; this booklet describes these and the legal and taxation implications of each and stresses the importance of making a correct choice at the outset.

Public companies: the way ahead. *Arthur Young, 70pp.*
The purpose of this book is twofold; first, to explore the principal factors that a public company should consider when developing its corporate objectives, and second, to summarise the options open to it and discuss their legal and tax implications. Topics covered are:

dealing with the public
responsibility of directors
corporate acquisitions
corporate divestment
finance for a public company
dealing with a takeover bid.

Thirty pages of appendices cover Stock Exchange and City code requirements and the company law implications of public company status.

Accountants' reports on profits forecasts. *Deloitte Haskins and Sells, 120pp.*
A detailed review of accountants' reports on profit forecasts, how they are undertaken and the regulatory framework under which they are issued. Useful for accountants and company directors alike.

Accountants' reports on takeovers, mergers, acquisitions and realisations. *Deloitte Haskins and Sells, 392pp.*
Prepared principally to guide accountants in the preparation of their reports, this substantial book would be of considerable use to company directors who need to understand their nature and purpose. Separate chapters cover the City code on takeovers and mergers, Stock Exchange and legal requirements and descriptions of how investigations and valuations are carried out.

Business advisory service series. *Peat Marwick Mitchell.*
A series of four-page leaflets providing background information on current business and management topics. Subjects covered include:

management buyouts
PAYE audits
government loan guarantee schemes
statutory sick pay
investment of liquid funds

financing private education
factoring
finance for exports
company cars.

Corporate audit committees: a guide for directors. *Ernst and Whinney, 25pp.*
Explains the functions and duties of audit committees and why they are considered necessary. Provides a guide to the type of questions that an effective audit committee should be asking management, internal auditors and external auditors.

Travel and entertainment expenses in British business. *American Express, 21pp.*
The results of two research projects conducted by American Express in 1984 and 1985 into the scale and control of travel and entertainment expenditure by UK companies indicate that, while these items cost considerably more than advertising and corporation tax put together, relatively little policy effort is put into their control. Discusses how these costs can be more effectively monitored and controlled.

Moving location. *Investors in Industry, 15pp.*
This booklet is written both for the chief executive faced with the decision whether or not to move business premises and for the managers subsequently involved in implementing a decision to move. The why, where, when and how of moving are covered and a useful list of sources of information and advice is provided.

Marketing: developing profitable business. *Investors in Industry, 15pp.*
This guide is intended primarily for the chief executive who wishes to review the future direction of his company, but would also be of considerable value to students of marketing or business strategy. Topics covered include identifying and exploiting opportunities, pricing and successful selling. An appendix describes some cost effective computer-based approaches to business planning.

Writing and reading a speech. *Deloitte Haskins and Sells, 38pp.*
This booklet should be compulsory reading in most companies;

it provides a valuable step-by-step guide to the preparation and delivery of an oral presentation. Particular attention is given to the development of an effective speaking style and helpful examples are provided.

Report writing. *Deloitte Haskins and Sells, Part I 92pp. and Part II 67pp.*
The two parts together provide a comprehensive course in report writing. All aspects are covered thoroughly and practical advice is given on style, structure and the selection of material.

Industry briefs. *National Westminster Bank, 4pp.*
A useful series of leaflets produced by the Market Intelligence Department at Natwest, each outlines the salient features of and recent trends in particular industry segments. Recent editions have covered:

retail trends
residential homes for the elderly
garden centres, nurseries and florists
catering
books, magazines and newspapers.

Chapter 6

Information and Advice for Smaller Businesses

Only rarely will those who establish a new business possess the full range of skills and experience needed to ensure its survival and growth. Typically they will be enthusiastic specialists who may not be proficient in such areas as financial control, administration and management. The publications listed in this chapter will, it is hoped, plug some of these gaps and assist small businessmen establish and develop their businesses.

General information

The government's Small Firms Service was administered by the Department of Trade and Industry when the leaflets mentioned below were prepared, but is now the responsibility of the Department of Employment. If you have any difficulty in obtaining the publications, dial the operator on 100 and ask for freefone Enterprise.

Your own business. *Arthur Young, 11 booklets.*
Each 5-6pp. booklet summarises or presents a checklist of the principal aspects of a subject concerning a smaller or newly established business. These subjects are:

- new business checklist
- sole trader, partnership or limited company?
- the duties of directors
- types of finance
- making a case for finance
- taxation and the new business
- value added tax
- employing people
- an introduction to pensions

an introduction to marketing
an introduction to insurance.

Helping high technology companies to grow. *Arthur Young, 12pp.*
A brief description of the four major stages of growth, ie start-up, development, consolidation and expansion. Identifies some of the problems encountered in the management of growth.

CoSIRA information pack. *Council for Small Industries in Rural Areas, 8 leaflets.*
The function of CoSIRA, an agency of the Development Commission, is to help small rural businesses in England to prosper. This information pack contains leaflets on:

functions of CoSIRA
practical assistance for small rural businesses
technical and business management advice
training
village shops
publications for small rural businesses
old building — new opportunities
the Development Commission.

Business survival. *KMG Thomson McLintock, 15pp.*
Deals with some of the things that can go wrong with a company and describes possible schemes of reconstruction to deal with them.

A big help to a small business. *Department of Trade and Industry, 3pp.*
Describes the facilities offered by the Small Firms Service. Its information service and first three counselling sessions are free.

Tendering for government contracts: advice for small firms. *Department of Trade and Industry, 27pp.*
Like all markets, the government procurement operation has its own features which need to be understood by the potential new supplier. This booklet assists the smaller business to enter this market by outlining the procedures and identifying the main buying agencies. A useful list of additional publications concerned with the more detailed aspects of selling to specific government departments is included.

Business advisory service. *Midland Bank, 6pp.*
Describes the Midland Bank's Business Advisory Service which provides customers with a detailed report on their business, free of charge.

The banks and small firms. *Banking Information Service, 23pp.*
Describes the role that the London and Scottish clearing banks play in meeting the financial needs of small firms. Chapters cover lending terms and conditions, special lending schemes, instalment credit and leasing, export finance, equity finance, support for high technology and advisory services. Special mention is made of co-operation with public sector bodies and an appendix sets out some recent developments in the banks' support for smaller firms.

Small business digest. *National Westminster Bank, occasional publication.*
This publication deals with matters of interest to the owners and managers of smaller businesses. For example, the October 1985 issue contained articles on:

enterprise agencies
bank charges explained
the elements of a successful business.

Directory of enterprise agencies and community action programmes. *Business in the Community, 56pp.*
Describes the role of the enterprise agencies and provides alphabetical and geographical lists of all the agencies in the UK. Each entry contains the address and telephone number of the agency, the name of the director and an indication of the facilities and services provided.

Management buy-outs. *KMG Thomson McLintock, 27pp.*
Management buy-outs are a relatively recent phenomenon and each one is different. This booklet explains how a buy-out situation might arise and discusses the commercial, financial, legal and taxation aspects.

Should you buy your company? *Robson Rhodes, 12pp.*
A similar publication to the one above. Buy-outs, and the circumstances under which they might be possible, are described and the financial, legal and tax aspects are covered.

Managing the growing business. *Spicer and Pegler, 40pp.* Aimed at those who run small businesses, this booklet deals with the problems and challenges met in the growth stages. Topics covered include cash planning, new product development, remuneration and reward policy. The final chapter concerns the realisation of the investment in a business, whether by outright sale, partial disposal or flotation.

The small businessman's guide to advertising and **The small businessman's guide to the media.** *Thomson Local Directories, 32 and 25pp. respectively.*
The first booklet describes the various forms of advertising and presents the pros and cons of each. The second examines each section of the media in depth.

Getting into business. *Arthur Andersen, 73pp.*
Concentrates on the major tax and financial factors to be considered when starting a business, particularly as regards the choice of business entity. The main chapters cover budgets and cash flow, sources of finance, administrative procedures and the calculation of taxable profits. The appendices include details of tax rates and allowances and a particularly useful worked example comparing the overall tax payable at various income levels by a sole trader, a partnership and a limited company.

Incorporating a business. *Pannell Kerr Forster, 24pp.*
Deals with two questions: should a new business venture be carried on through a company? The pros and cons of transforming an existing business into a company. The booklet focuses on taxation and contains 18 worked examples. A complex subject is presented clearly and concisely.

Starting your own business. *Lloyds Bank, 22pp.*
Advice for those trying to decide whether or not to set up in business and guidance for those who have decided to set up or have recently done so. Covers the basics well, and leads on to . . .

Making a small business bigger. *Lloyds Bank, 25pp.*
Starts with the question 'why make a small business bigger?' and goes on to discuss the problems of growth and the techniques needed to deal with them. Finance, planning and the presentation of proposals for investment are given special mention.

Setting up in business

Start up and go with Natwest. *National Westminster Bank, 26pp.*
A clear and concise introductory booklet which covers marketing, legal questions, money and administration and employing people. Includes a section on self-assessment, an action checklist and a selection of useful addresses and telephone numbers.

Starting up your own business. *Investors in Industry, 15pp.*
A lively and informative booklet set out in three main sections: the idea, the money and the people. The appendices outline the legal and financial aspects and provide a checklist to assist with thinking the project through.

Starting in business. *Kidsons, 11pp.*
Brief and readable, this booklet consists of 11 one-page chapters on each of the main areas for consideration.

Starting your own business — the practical steps. *Department of Trade and Industry, 15pp.*
Describes the various types of business — sole traders, partnerships, companies and co-operatives — and covers National Insurance, taxation, premises and insurance. The booklet also refers to other free DTI publications and to the Small Firms Service business counsellor who provides free initial consultations.

Financial planning and control

Elements of book-keeping. *Department of Trade and Industry, 15pp.*
Book-keeping is an important business skill and this useful booklet outlines the elements, provides worked examples and makes helpful practical points.

Understanding your annual accounts. *Bank of Scotland, 19pp.*
A well-written summary of what accounts are, what they mean and how the businessman can use them. Useful explanations of

working capital, source and application of funds statements and use of financial ratios.

Financial planning and control. *Midland Bank, 28pp.*
Stresses the importance of financial planning in the control of a business and covers profit and loss accounts budgets, cash flow forecasts and the control of creditors, debtors and stocks. Good illustrations complement the clear text.

Planning profit and loss and cash flow. *National Westminster Bank, 22pp.*
A clear and lively explanation of how to prepare and use profit and cash flow plans. Contains excellent worked examples. Concludes with advice on how to present a case to a bank manager. Some blank cash flow forecast planning sheets are contained in the back pocket.

Financial control in the smaller business. *Binder Hamlyn, 17pp.*
Stresses the importance of the trading and financing cycles in a business, and explains the role of financial control in the context of these cycles. Good diagrams and useful checklists covering cash, stock and work in progress, debtors, creditors, assets employed and capital structure.

Financial control in a privately-owned business. *Ernst and Whinney, 16pp.*
Starts with the development of the business plan then considers how the plan is monitored and how corrective action is taken. Clear diagrams.

Improving your financial control. *Bank of Scotland, 23pp.*
Covers profit and loss account budgets, management reports and cash flow forecasting and contains useful practical advice on the control of debtors.

Budgetary control in the smaller company. *Investors in Industry, 19pp.*
Stresses that the purpose of budgetary control is to enable the proprietors of a company to delegate; it is, therefore, an important catalyst for growth. Explains the nature of budgetary control and how it operates. A series of appendices provide excellent examples of statements and reports which might be

produced by such a system.

Pricing and costing. *Investors in Industry, 28pp.*
This critical subject is tackled in a clear and comprehensive way. The importance of pricing in relation to profitability is stressed at the outset and various pricing strategies are discussed including tactical pricing. Costing principles and methods are explained and demonstrated and the appendices include a glossary of costing terms.

Business planning

Running your own business — planning for success. *Department of Trade and Industry, 22pp.*
A basic guide to planning for newly established businesses, this booklet contains checklists designed to identify the plans and decisions which are likely to be critical to the success of the small business.

Business plan. *KMG Thomson McLintock.*
Five checklists cover the elements of a business plan: cash control, presenting a business plan, management accounts and information systems, budgeting and marketing.

Outline for a new venture business plan. *Arthur Young, 11pp.*
Summarises the need for a business plan and the items to be included in it. A series of questions are posed the answers to which comprise the main points to be included in any business plan. A suggested plan structure is included in an appendix.

Corporate strategy. *Moores and Rowland, 15pp.*
Outlines the aims and processes of corporate planning, under the following headings:

why plan?
where is the company now?
where does the company want to be?
which way to get there?
what to do on arrival?

Production management

Production controls in the smaller manufacturing company. *Investors in Industry, 28pp.*
This excellent description of the main control functions in a manufacturing company covers marketing, production, financial and personnel aspects. The clear text is supplemented by good illustrations, particularly in the appendices which provide examples of basic control documentation. There is a useful bibliography.

Managing manufacturing in the smaller company. *Investors in Industry, 24pp.*
Covers the tasks and responsibilities of manufacturing management and offers advice and guidance on such matters as organisation, customer relations, fixed asset management, procurement, administration, information and control, industrial relations and quality control.

Chapter 7

Legal Matters

Most businessmen recognise the complications of the legal systems operating in the various parts of the United Kingdom and seek qualified legal advice before taking any significant decision. However, the general reader can get a grip of the most commonly encountered aspects of business law by reading some of the publications listed below.

Company law

Accounting problems of the Companies Acts. *Deloitte Haskins and Sells, 123pp.*
This excellent book is based on Deloitte's experience of handling their clients' difficulties in applying the accounting provisions of recent company legislation, much of which is based on European concepts and practices. It proceeds logically through the balance sheet and profit and loss account formats and contents and discusses such thorny problems as realised profits and modified financial statements. Contains a detailed index. Useful for students as well as businessmen and their advisers.

The Companies Act 1981: a guide to its requirements. *Arthur Young, 56pp.*
Covering similar ground to the above publication, this booklet includes examples of the standard profit and loss account and balance sheet formats. Contains a useful glossary of terms.

The accounting requirements of the Companies Act 1981. *Hodgson Impey, 35pp.*
A more summarised version, set out in a staccato, note-type style. The appendices contain the formats and a worked example.

The Companies Act 1985. *KMG Thomson McLintock, 84pp.*
Another superb publication from Thomson McLintock which covers the subject in depth. The main sections are:

amendments to previous legislation
problem areas in the legislation
directors' transactions
acquisition by a company of its own shares
prospectuses
table of cross-references between the old and new legislation
financial statements checklist.

A detailed index is included.

A guide to the Companies Act 1985. *Price Waterhouse, 32pp.*
Brief but comprehensive, this booklet, with the help of an extensive checklist, deals with the accounting and financial disclosures aspects of the 1985 Act.

Company accounting, disclosure and employment law.
Deloitte Haskins and Sells, 27pp.
This booklet, aimed primarily at persons and companies considering establishing a business in the UK, provides background information on company law, employment law and consumer protection law.

Businesses — who owns them? *Department of Trade and Industry, 3pp.*
Explains the Companies Acts requirement that owners of any business not carried on under their own names display the particulars of ownership on the premises and on their business stationery.

Financial and accounting responsibilities of directors.
Consultative Committee of Accountancy Bodies, 36pp.
A detailed and comprehensive publication (one of the CCAB's 'Technical Release' series) covering the civil and criminal law aspects of directors' responsibilities to their companies, to shareholders and to third parties.

Criminal liability of company directors. *Glaisyers, 12pp.*
A brief résumé of the principal areas where dishonesty or negligence can involve company directors with the criminal law.

Topics covered include health and safety, road traffic offences, the Consumer Credit Act and winding up a company.

Being public. *Ernst and Whinney, 28pp.*
Outlines the continuing responsibilities of public limited companies (PLCs) and their directors, as laid down by company law and the provisions of the City Code on Takeovers and Mergers and by the requirements of the Stock Exchange. Particular attention is given to the prohibitions on transactions with directors and insider dealing.

Consumer protection

The substantial body of consumer protection law is administered by the Office of Fair Trading which publishes a wide range of free booklets. A selection of the main titles is given below:

Buying by post
Cars
Dear shopper in Northern Ireland
Dear shopper in Scotland
Double glazing
Electrical goods
Estate agency: a guide to the Estate Agents Act 1979
Furniture
Home improvements
How to cope with doorstep salesmen
How to put things right
I'm taking it further! — Arbitration under codes of practice
Launderers and dry cleaners
Motorbikes
No credit?
Photography
Shoes
Shop around for credit

A general booklet **Office of Fair Trading: how it works** is also available.

A trader's guide. *Central Office of Information, 11pp.*
This useful leaflet outlines the law relating to the supply of goods and services. It provides guidance on such topics as the definition of 'merchantable quality', manufacturers' guarantees and contracting out of the liability.

Restrictive practices. *Office of Fair Trading, 51pp.*
Describes how certain types of agreement which restrict the action of the parties to the agreement must be registered in order to comply with the Restrictive Trade Practices Act 1976. The range of registrable agreements is considerably wider than might be thought and this publication provides detailed guidance on the law and its associated practice.

Consumer and business credit

Extending credit to customers, both retail and commercial, involves legal as well as business considerations. A successful credit policy will, therefore, require that the legal aspects are explicitly incorporated and most of the following publications concern the impact of the law on this aspect of business management.

Licensing. *Office of Fair Trading, 26pp.*
Under the Consumer Credit Act 1974 licences are required for the various activities of the consumer credit industry. This booklet explains who needs to apply for a licence, describes the licensing system and provides detailed guidance about the categories of licence.

Responsibilities of a licensee. *Office of Fair Trading, 14pp.*
Sets out what a licence under the Consumer Credit Act allows a licensee to do and how he is affected by the licensing system.

Regulated and exempt agreements. *Office of Fair Trading, 16pp.*
Expanding on the guidance contained in the booklet *Licensing*, this publication concentrates on regulated and exempt agreements. Useful decision diagram assists the reader to determine whether an agreement is an exempt 'debtor-supplier-creditor' agreement.

Extortionate credit. *Office of Fair Trading, 8pp.*
Explains the safeguards protecting consumers from extortionate levels of interest.

A guide to the consumer credit tables. *Office of Fair Trading, 9pp.*
Explains how the annual percentage rate (APR) is calculated from the relevant consumer credit table.

Credit charge. *Office of Fair Trading, 21pp.*
A more detailed and comprehensive explanation of the calculation of the annual percentage rate of interest and the rules relating to the advertising of interest charges.

Guidance for credit reference agencies. *Office of Fair Trading, 24pp.*
Explains the obligations placed on credit reference agencies by the Consumer Credit Act 1974. A useful table shows the stages and the time limits in the disputes procedure.

Hire agreements. *Office of Fair Trading, 22pp.*
Covers the provisions of the Consumer Credit Act relating to hire agreements and points out the consequences of failure to comply with the Act's requirements.

Cancellable agreements and **Non-cancellable agreements.** *Office of Fair Trading, 40 and 21pp. respectively.*
These two booklets explain the statutory requirements in respect of both cancellable and non-cancellable agreements and stress the legal difficulties resulting from non-compliance.

Matters arising during the lifetime of an agreement. *Office of Fair Trading, 23pp.*
Covers default and early settlement and explains the general duty to give various items of information. The decision diagrams add to the clarity of the text.

Advertising and quotations regulations. *Office of Fair Trading, 18pp.*
Explains the regulations which control advertisements offering credit or hire facilities.

About instalment credit. *Finance Houses Association, 20pp.*
A general, non-technical explanation of how instalment credit works and the various kinds of arrangement under which

it is provided.

Consumers and debt. *Finance Houses Association, 14pp.*
Discusses problem areas connected with consumer debt. Explains how credit decisions are made and problems regarding payment dealt with. The final section includes checklists, for the providers and users of consumer debt services, which are designed to help avoid some of these problems.

Debt collection services. *Glaisyers, 8pp.*
Describes how the payment of overdue debts is enforced by means of a court order and outlines the possible courses of action against defaulting individuals and companies.

A guide to credit scoring. *Finance Houses Association, 8pp.*
A recent development in the consumer finance industry has been the introduction of 'credit scoring' by major lenders and it seems likely that this technique will become more widespread in the future. This booklet explains how the technique of assessing the statistical probability that a debt will be repaid works in practice.

Managing the credit risk. *Arthur Andersen, 15pp.*
This brief guide to the law and practice of insolvency outlines a number of practical steps which can be taken to avoid or mitigate some of the effects of customer insolvency.

A banker's guide to survival: what to do with problem accounts. *Price Waterhouse, 15pp.*
Explains that there are many options available to a creditor who finds himself with a problem account on his hands. Advice is given on spotting the danger signs, receivership, security and dealing with a liquidation.

Health and safety

The Health and Safety Executive produces a long list of publications on health and safety law:

Advice to employers
Advice to the self-employed

Asbestos and you
Code of safety at fairs
Control of dust in the cotton textile industry
Danger: fires and heaters need air
Dirt and disease
Dust
Electrical equipment certification service
Farmer's lung
Fires and explosions due to the misuse of oxygen
First aid provision in small workplaces
Guidance on the implementation of safety policies
Handling pesticides
New regulations for packaging and labels for dangerous substances
Respiratory diseases in the mushroom industry
A short guide to the 1974 Act
Writing a policy statement: advice to employers

The Executive also provides technical or interpretive advice through its area information services (see booklet **Area office information services**).

Employment and industrial relations law

The Department of Employment has produced a number of publications on employment legislation:

Employees' rights on insolvency of employers
Employment rights for the expectant mother
Employment rights on the transfer of an undertaking
Facing redundancy? Time off for job hunting or to arrange training
Guarantee payments
Itemized pay statements
Procedure for handling redundancies
Redundancy payments
Rights on termination of employment
Rules governing continuous employment and a week's pay
Suspension on medical grounds under health and safety regulations
Time off for public duties
Unfairly dismissed?
Union membership rights and the closed shop
Union secret ballots
Written statement of main terms and conditions of employment

The Department's other publications include:

Code of practice: closed shop agreements and arrangements
Code of practice: picketing
Fair and unfair dismissal: a guide for employers

Individual rights of employees: a guide for employers
Industrial tribunal procedure
The law on unfair dismissal: a guide for small firms

A guide to the Trade Union Act 1984. *Department of Employment, 24pp.*
Covers the election of union leaders, ballots before industrial action and political contributions. Designed to make both the union member and employer aware of the rights and duties conferred by this legislation.

Industrial action and the law. *Department of Employment, 15pp.*
Gives the reader a general understanding of how the law applies to industrial action. Covers the immunity of unions and instances when immunity does not apply, and includes sections on secondary industrial action.

Employed or self-employed? *Hodgson Impey, 8pp.*
It is often important to determine whether a person is employed by another or is self-employed, not only for employment law purposes but also for tax and National Insurance purposes. This technical bulletin outlines the law on the subject and provides a checklist to assist in applying the legal tests.

Planning law

Planning permission: a guide for industry. *Department of the Environment, 47pp.*
This guide is intended to explain the planning control system to the potential industrial developer and to help him submit an application for planning permission. The appendices include a useful planning chart indicating the different stages and how long each is likely to take.

Land compensation: your rights explained. *Department of the Environment.*
The five booklets in this series cover the compensation and other benefits which may be available if property is affected by public works. Each one deals briefly with the what, how and when of compensation in a clear and concise manner and

indicates when advice may be required on, for example, development land tax.

The farmer and public development
Insulation against traffic noise
Your business and public development
Your home and compulsory purchase
Your home and nuisance from public development

Personal legal matters

A simple guide to divorce. *Kenwright and Cox, 11pp.*
Guidance on the procedures of divorce and on how the divorce will affect the couple's financial situation and the children of the marriage.

Tax and divorce. *Kenwright and Cox, 22pp.*
This is a companion booklet to the one above and deals with the tax aspects of separation and divorce. Particular attention is paid to methods of minimising income tax and National Insurance payments, subjects which may easily be overlooked.

Financial aspects of separation and divorce. *Neville Russell, 30pp.*
Covers not only tax and National Insurance but also provides guidance on wills, pensions, life assurance and the effects of remarriage. The appendices contain tax and National Insurance rates and checklists of income and expenditure and assets and liabilities.

Wills and trusts. *Barclays Bank, 9pp.*
A brief description of the why and how of making a will and of creating a trust under a will. While this booklet is clearly an advertisement for Barclays Bank Trust Company, it contains useful information on what executors can and cannot do and how much it will cost to appoint the bank as the executor.

Solicitors: accounting for clients' and trust money. *Dearden Farrow, 12pp.*
Describes the Solicitors' Accounts Rules for handling and

accounting for clients' money. This is a subject of considerable interest to individuals as well as to solicitors since the latter are often in possession of a person's entire wealth, even if only for a short period.

Chapter 8

Computers

Choosing a business computer and software without professional advice is probably one of the most difficult — and risky — areas of management today. The information listed below will enable the businessman to make a better informed choice.

Computer selection and installation

Microcomputers for the privately-owned business. *Ernst and Whinney; 28pp.*
A useful introductory booklet which explains briefly what a microcomputer is, what it will and will not do and how to go about acquiring and installing one successfully.

A guide for potential computer users. *KMG Thomson McLintock, 24pp.*
This booklet has two parts, the first covering choosing a computer and the second describing computer terminology and services.

How to select and install a small business computer. *Dearden Farrow, 34pp.*
Explains clearly using a step-by-step approach how to choose a business computer. Describes the feasibility study and progresses through systems design and selection to implementation. A useful 12-page glossary of computer terminology is included.

Choosing the right computer. *Investors in Industry, 16pp.*
Aimed at the small to medium-sized company, this booklet covers specification, selection and implementation, and contains a useful series of checklists for each stage.

Computers: negotiating the contract. *Investors in Industry, 24pp.*
A companion booklet to the one above, this publication looks at the computer purchase and service agreement from the customer's angle. The text covers the main steps from supplier selection to post-implementation support, and the appendices contain checklists of the points to be covered in a wide variety of computer contracts.

Information technology. *Investors in Industry, 20pp.*
Provides an overview of the range of information technology from data and word processing systems to telecommunications, computer assisted design and manufacturing (CAD and CAM) and the electronic office. Good diagrams, glossary and cartoons by McLachlan.

Office automation — a manager's guide. *Arthur Andersen, 41pp.*
A useful summary of this rapidly developing subject. The booklet falls into three sections: some common questions about office automation, an introduction to the key technologies and case studies (Department of Trade and Industry, Plessey, the BBC and Willis Faber).

Data Protection Act

The Data Protection Act came into force in November 1985 and affects anyone who holds or automatically processes any personal data.

The Data Protection Act 1984: guideline No. 1. *Data Protection Registrar, 24pp.*
The first of a series of guidelines published by the Data Protection Registrar and dealing with the principles of the Act and the mechanics of registration, this one introduces the Act, describes its main provisions and offers guidance for data users and computer bureaux. Future guidelines will cover:

definitions
registration process
data protection principles

individuals' rights
exemptions
enforcement and appeals
computer bureaux
timetable.

The Data Protection Act 1984: questions and answers (1-20). *Data Protection Registrar, 16pp.*
Illustrates the provisions of the Act in question-and-answer form.

The Data Protection Act: notes to help you apply for registration. *Data Protection Registrar, 45pp.*
Explains the registration process and guides applicants in the completion of the formalities.

Guide to the Data Protection Act 1984. *Arthur Andersen, 15pp.*
A brief overview of the provisions of the Act and its likely impact on business.

The Data Protection Act: does it affect you? *Ernst and Whinney, 15pp.*
Presented as a series of questions such as 'Do I have to register?' and 'What are my obligations after registering?'. Particularly useful.

Chapter 9

Investment

The Stock Exchange. *The Stock Exchange, 17pp.*
A useful and informative introduction to the functions and operations of the Stock Exchange. Explains the need for a securities market, describes the detailed workings of the Stock Exchange from the point of view of the investor and of the company whose shares are listed. Ends with an excellent glossary.

An introduction to buying and selling shares. *The Stock Exchange, 17pp.*
A simplified version of the preceding publication. Contains sections on understanding the city pages and the Financial Times index and a brief discussion of taxation.

The gilt-edged market. *The Stock Exchange, 15pp.*
Companion volume to the one above. Explains in a clear and straightforward manner the background to the issue of government securities and how they are traded.

A simple guide to traded options. *The Stock Exchange, 19pp.*
A useful guide to this recent development in the stock market, produced as a companion volume to the above two publications.

A number of video tapes are available on free hire from the Stock Exchange in VHS, Betamax or Sony-U-Matic formats:

My word is my bond *(18 minutes).*
Shows the importance of the Stock Exchange as a national institution and the way its activities affect, directly or indirectly, two out of three people in this country.

The Stock Exchange and you *(20 minutes).*
Designed for potential private investors, explains the various services provided by stockbrokers.

The Unlisted Securities Market *(18 minutes).*
Takes two fictitious companies and analyses their reasons for wishing to join the USM; explains its advantages for small or medium-sized companies.

The gilt-edged market *(18 minutes).*
Aimed at older students and adults, explains the workings and economic reasoning behind the functions of the market in gilt-edged securities and the work of the Government Broker.

Introduction to traded options *(14 minutes).*
Introduces the new investor to the traded options market, explaining briefly how it works with particular attention to call options.

Traded puts *(21 minutes).*
Following on from the above tape, this video treats traded put options in more detail.

Call options in action *(18 minutes).*
Provides a more practical explanation of call options, showing how to use the market rather than dealing with the theories behind it.

Investing in National Savings: a reference guide for professional advisers. *Department for National Savings, 63pp.*
Provides detailed information on the full range of National Savings products. Part I describes each of the savings products, its tax implications and special features. Part II provides background information on, eg savings for children and overseas residents and what to do when a saver dies. A full list is provided of the gilt-edged stock on the National Savings Stock Register and the dates on which interest is paid on each.

More for your money. *Association of Investment Trust Companies, 28pp.*
Explains what investment trust companies are and how they work. Points out the difference between investment trusts and unit trusts and describes the favourable tax treatment of unit trusts. Included in the appendices is a description of the investment trust table published each month in the *Financial Times* and the *Daily Telegraph* and how to read it.

An investor's guide to the Business Expansion Scheme. *Clark Whitehill, 23pp.*
Describes the scheme and how it works, with particular attention to the tax advantages and the potential returns available to the investor. Includes a useful section on the mechanics of obtaining tax relief together with a description of how the relief may be subject to clawback and how it interacts with capital gains tax.

An introduction to Lloyd's underwriting. *Hodgson Impey, 18pp.*
Describes for the potential underwriting member of Lloyd's the requirements and consequences of membership and explains the tax implications. Ends with a clear and timely warning about the risks of membership.

Currency options. *Arthur Andersen, 20pp.*
Describes the accounting and taxation aspects of currency option investment and contains a useful section on controlling risk.

Investing in gold. *Heinold Commodities, 9pp.*
Written principally with the US investor in mind but applicable to UK conditions. Quotes examples of investment in rising and falling scenarios and advises on how to choose between the five principal mechanisms for investing in gold.

Gold and silver. *Heinold Commodities, 12pp.*
Describes recent trends in the gold, silver and platinum markets and advises on future investment strategy.

Eurobonds: a guide for investors. *Barclays Merchant Bank, 20pp.*
Eurobonds can offer the investor an attractive, secure and ascertainable return. Describes what Eurobonds are and explains the workings of the market and the mechanics of trading. Provides a comprehensive glossary.

Options on currency futures: an introduction and **Options on Eurodollar futures: an introduction.** *Chicago Mercantile Exchange, 20pp. each.*
These booklets explain the fundamentals of two of the more exotic investment media available to international investors. Each provides enough detail to enable the diligent reader to

understand the nature of the investment and how to trade and refers to additional material available from the Chicago Mercantile Exchange office in London.

Investing in United States real estate. *Kenneth Leventhal and Co, 24pp.*
An overview for non-US investors of the real estate market in the USA. Covers the market sectors, financing and tax aspects.

A guide to buying property in Spain. *Glaisyers, 8pp.*
A brief introductory guide to the legal, taxation and financial aspects of buying a Spanish property. Also touches on residence and wills.

Annual bullion review. *Samuel Montagu, 45pp.*
Written for the serious bullion investor, this publication analyses recent prices and production levels of gold, silver and platinum. The comprehensive and detailed commentaries trace the effects of economic and political events on the markets. Tables show the London bullion prices for each trading day for the previous year.

A short guide to the London international financial futures exchange. *Peat Marwick Mitchell, 55pp.*
Explains the general nature of financial futures and the operation of the market. Shows how the market can be used for risk management. Covers accounting, taxation and internal control aspects.

The serious investor's guide to the world of futures. *Metaport Commodities, 12pp.*
Explains briefly the nature of the commodity futures markets and how investors can operate in them.

Investing in forestry. *Neville Russell, 3pp.*
Investing in new forestry developments and in mature woodlands can be very attractive, especially for the higher-rate taxpayer. This leaflet describes the government assistance available and how the profits from forestry are taxed.

Chapter 10

Miscellaneous

Property

All businesses need accommodation and the cost of providing it, whether it is owned or rented, is a major component in most budgets. Equally, property development and investment in established property is a large and important business activity in most of the developed economies. The publications reviewed below cover both aspects of this subject.

World rental levels: offices. *Richard Ellis, 4pp.*
This short publication contains a great deal of condensed information about office rental and other accommodation costs in 21 cities of the world. Graphical trend information covering the last 15 years is provided for many of these cities.

UK property report. *Richard Ellis, 19pp.*
This detailed review of the property market is produced annually and covers the industrial, commercial and residential sectors. Contains a comprehensive list of the firm's free publications, some of which are described in this section.

City of London office review. *Richard Ellis, 6pp.*
Another annual report which describes the supply and demand patterns in office accommodation in the City of London. Rental trends are outlined and explained and the short-term outlook is analysed.

West End office report. *Richard Ellis, 6pp.*
Covers rent levels, location preferences and the composition of the tenant population. There are parallel publications on Bristol, Reading and Manchester.

Suburban London offices: the occupiers' view. *Richard Ellis, 12pp.*
Analyses the responses to a survey carried out by Richard Ellis

in 1984 among the occupiers of suburban London offices. Describes the background to the survey and discusses its results, with particular reference to participants' reasons for moving from central London to the suburbs, and their implications for the office property market.

The impact of the microchip on the demand for offices. *Richard Ellis, 15pp.*
This thoughtful and detailed research report is important reading for any businessman whose operations are likely to be affected by the microchip.

Property in the United Kingdom. *Clark Whitehill, 15pp.*
A guide for individuals and companies considering property development or investing in established UK property. Provides background information on residential and commercial property development and information on sources of finance, taxation and planning.

Property rent indices and market editorial (PRIME). *Healey and Baker, 22pp.*
Contains details of trends in retail, office and industrial rentals throughout Great Britain and provides an assessment of the trends in office and industrial rentals in each of the main regions.

Investment report. *Healey and Baker, 4pp.*
Provides clear geographical analyses of commercial property yields over the last 15 years versus the returns on comparable investments and bank base rates.

The MLP-CIG property index. *Michael Laurie and Partners, 16pp.*
This detailed report compares yields on investments in various types of property in the UK and the USA. The total return from property investment is usefully analysed between capital growth and rental income. Summarised trends in UK average rents and capital values are also given.

Commercial property and the rating system: a fair deal for all? *Herring Son and Daw, 6pp.*
Summarises the results of a research project which examined how the commercial rating system might be replaced by a

uniform business tax, based on property capital values. The report concludes that the main winners from such a change would be industrial occupiers in the Midlands and the North and the main losers would be freehold owners and occupiers of central city stores in the South.

Pensions

Money matters special report on personal pensions. *Sun Alliance, video tape (18 minutes).*
Provides an introduction to personal pensions for the self-employed, differentiating between conventional, unit-linked and index-linked plans, and explains how each can meet a different pension need.

Money matters special report on directors' and executives' pensions. *Sun Alliance, video tape (18 minutes).*
Explains and demonstrates with some typical figures how a pension plan for directors of small companies can provide tax-efficient security in retirement. Explains loan back facilities and draws the distinction between managed and self-administered schemes. Stresses the importance of seeking advice from impartial and skilled pensions consultants and of starting pension planning as early as possible.

NB There is also a 12-page booklet published by Sun Alliance, covering much the same ground as this tape, which takes the example of a small building firm and its directors.

Retirement annuity policies. *Clark Whitehill, 4pp.*
Provides an *aide-mémoire* of the principal features of personal pension plans as regards eligibility, tax benefits, levels of contribution and the range of benefits available on retirement.

Small self-administered pension schemes. *Clark Whitehill, 4pp.*
A companion leaflet to the one above explaining briefly what self-administered pension schemes are and how they are set up, and examining the tax advantages.

Pension news. *Stewart Wrightson, 8pp.*
A newsletter providing regular, up-to-date information and

comment on matters affecting occupational and state pension schemes. Very useful background for any businessman who needs to take more than a passing interest in the subject.

Insurance

Most insurance companies and many banks provide informative literature on the various types of insurance and the risks that each covers. A brief sample selection is provided below.

A businessman's guide to liability insurance. *Sun Alliance, 12pp.*
Outlines a businessman's duty of care to his employees and to the public and explains how the liabilities arising from it can be insured.

Straightforward business protection. *Sun Alliance, 11pp.*
Explains how a variety of insurances covering liabilities, damage and business losses of all kind can be included in a composite policy. Includes a checklist for assessing the values to be insured.

Assets and earnings insurance. *Sun Alliance, 6pp.*
Explains briefly how insurance can protect both business assets and the profits that would otherwise be lost if the assets were damaged or destroyed.

Office insurance. *Sun Alliance, 8pp.*
Describes insurable risks and the cover that can be provided against them.

Security at risk. *Sun Alliance, 12pp.*
A short guide to the physical security of property and money, including a useful section on alarms and signalling equipment.

Personal protection. *Sun Alliance, 12pp.*
The illness, injury or death of an employee can be expensive for a business. This guide outlines the protection it can take against these eventualities.

Sun Alliance insurance handbook for solicitors. *Sun Alliance, 16pp.*
Advice to solicitors on how they can protect themselves and their clients. Contains a comprehensive résumé of practice cover, personal insurances and pensions and the provision of indemnities.

Insurance: could your present insurance repair the damage? *Barclays Bank, 16pp.*
Basically a warning against under-insurance, this booklet identifies the main types of domestic insurance and explains what they cover and what they cost.

United Kingdom glossary of insurance terms. *Ernst and Whinney, 42pp.*
Clear and concise definitions of hundreds of terms, from A1 to Zillmer, used on the London insurance market. An appendix lists abbreviations and acronyms.

Unusual risks. *Risk Management Consultants Ltd in collaboration with the British Insurance Brokers Association, 34pp.*
Written primarily for insurance brokers, this booklet describes some of the less common forms of insurance and lists the insurers who can provide cover.

Social security

The Department of Health and Social Security (DHSS) publishes a wide range of leaflets for claimants, employers and advisers on the many aspects of social security. Most of these are available from post offices and local DHSS offices. The titles are generally self-explanatory and a list of some of the most useful is set out below:

CH1	*Child benefit*
CH4	*Child benefit for children away from home*
CH4a	*Children in the care of a local authority*
CH5	*Child benefit for people entering Britain*
CH6	*Child benefit for people leaving Britain*
CH7	*Child benefit for children aged 16 and over*
CH11	*One-parent families*

D11	*NHS dental treatment — what it costs and how to get free treatment*
D49	*What to do after a death*
FB2	*Which benefit?*
FB5	*Social security: service families going abroad*
FB8	*Babies and benefits*
FB9	*Unemployed?*
FB15	*Injured at work: a guide to cash benefits*
FB18	*Long-term sick and disabled: cash help for people at home*
FB20	*Leaving school? A pocket guide to social security*
FIS1	*Family income supplement*
G11	*National health glasses*
H11	*Fares to hospital*
HB1	*Help for handicapped people*
MV11	*Free milk and vitamins*
NI2	*Industrial injuries: prescribed industrial diseases*
NI6	*Industrial injuries: disablement benefit and increases*
N19	*Going into hospital?: what happens to your social security benefit or pension?*
NI12	*Unemployment benefit*
NI14	*Guardian's allowance*
NI16a	*Invalidity benefit*
NI38	*Social security abroad*
NI49	*Death grant*
NI55	*Unemployment benefit for seasonal workers*
NI93	*Child's special allowance*
NI125	*Training for further employment and your NI record*
NI196	*Social security benefit rates*
NI205	*Attendance allowance*
NI207	*Occupational deafness*
NI212	*Invalid care allowance*
NI229	*Christmas bonus*
NI230	*Unemployment benefit and your occupational pension*
NI231	*Made redundant?*
NI237	*Occupational asthma*
NI240	*Voluntary work and social security benefits*
NI241	*Industrial injury benefit*
NI242	*Part-time work and social security benefits*
NI243	*Mobility allowance: payment directly into bank or building society accounts*
NI246	*How to appeal*
NI247	*Living together as husband and wife*
NI248	*Social security: new ways of claiming for couples*
NI251	*Attendance allowance: payment directly into bank or building society accounts*
NI252	*Severe disablement allowance*
NP12	*Social security: school leavers and students*
NP35	*Your benefit as a widow*
NP36	*Your benefit as a widow after the first 26 weeks*
P11	*NHS prescriptions: how to get them free*
RR1	*Who pays less rent and rates?*

SB1	*Cash help: supplementary benefits*
SB2	*Supplementary benefit: strikes and trade disputes*
SB7	*Supplementary benefit: living together as husband and wife*
SB8	*Supplementary benefit for pensioners, sick and disabled people, single parents and others not signing on as unemployed*
SB9	*Supplementary benefit for unemployed people*
SB16	*Lump sum payments*
SB17	*Help with heating costs*
SB18	*Supplementary benefit: the capital rule*
SB19	*Supplementary benefit: weekly payments for special needs*
SB21	*Cash help*

Chapter 11

Names and Addresses of Providers of Information

Allied Dunbar Assurance plc, Allied Dunbar Centre, Swindon SN1 1EL

American Express, 2-3 Cursitor Street, London EC4A 1LX

ANZ Banking Corporation plc, 55 Gracechurch Street, London EC3V 0BN

Armitage and Norton, PO Box A10, Station Street Buildings, Huddersfield HD1 1LZ

Arthur Andersen and Co, 2 Surrey Street, London WC2R 2PS

Arthur Young and Co, Rolls House, 7 Rolls Buildings, Fetter Lane, London EC4A 1NH

Association of Investment Trust Companies, Park House (6th Floor), 16 Finsbury Circus, London EC2M 7JJ

Banco di Roma SpA, 14-18 Eastcheap, London EC3M 1JY

Banking Information Service, 10 Lombard Street, London EC3V 0AR

Bank of Ireland plc, 36 Moorgate, London EC2R 6DP

Bank of Scotland, The Mound, Edinburgh EH1 1YZ

Banque Nationale de Paris plc, 8-13 King William Street, London EC4P 4HS

Barclays Bank plc, 54 Lombard Street, London EC3P 3AH

Barclays Merchant Bank Ltd, 15-16 Gracechurch Street, London EC3V 0BA

Binder Hamlyn and Co, 8 St Bride Street, London EC4A 4DA

British Bank of the Middle East, 99 Bishopsgate, London EC2P 2LA

British Overseas Trade Board, 1 Victoria Street, London SW1H 0ET

Business International, 12-14 chemin Rieu, 1208 Geneva, Switzerland

Business in the Community, 227A City Road, London EC1V ILX

Central Office of Information, Hercules Road, London SE1 7DU

Charterhouse Japhet plc, 1 Paternoster Row, London EC4M 7DH

Chicago Mercantile Exchange, 27 Throgmorton Street, London EC2N 2AN

Citibank NA, Citibank House, 336 Strand, London WC2R 1HB

Clark Whitehill and Co, 25 New Street Square, London EC4A 3LN

Consultative Committee of Accountancy Bodies, PO Box 433 Chartered Accountants' Hall, Moorgate Place, London EC2P 2BJ

Coopers and Lybrand, Plumtree Court, London EC4A 4HT

Council for Small Industries in Rural Areas, 141 Castle Street, Salisbury SP1 3TP

HM Customs and Excise, VAT Administration Directorate, King's Beam House, 39-41 Mark Lane, London EC3R 7HE

Data Protection Registrar, Springfield House, Water Lane, Wilmslow, Cheshire SK9 5AX

Dearden Farrow, 1 Serjeants Inn, London EC4Y 1JD

Deloitte Haskins and Sells, PO Box 207, 128 Queen Victoria Street, London EC4P 4JX

Department of Employment, Information Division, Caxton House, Tothill Street, London SW1H 9NF

English Tourist Board, 4 Grosvenor Gardens, London SW1W 0DU

Department of the Environment, Information Division, 2 Marsham Street, London SW1P 3EB

Ernst and Whinney, Becket House, Lambeth Palace Road, London SE1 7EU

Export Credits Guarantee Department, PO Box 272, Aldermanbury House, Aldermanbury, London EC2P 2EL

Finance Houses Association, 18 Upper Grosvenor Street, London W1X 9PB

Forward Trust Group, Broad Street House, 55 Old Broad Street, London EC2M 1RX

Glaisyers, Alpha Tower, Suffolk Street, Birmingham B1 1TR

Greater Manchester Economic Development Corporation (GMEDC), Bernhard House, Piccadilly Gardens, Manchester M1 4DD

Hacker Young and Co, St Alphage House, Fore Street, London EC2Y 5DH

Healey and Baker, 29 Saint George Street, Hanover Square, London W1A 3BG

Health and Safety Executive, Regina House, 259-69 Old Marylebone Road, London NW1 5RR

Department of Health and Social Security, Information Division, Alexander Fleming House, Elephant and Castle, London SE1 6BY

Heinold Commodities Ltd, Plantation House, Mincing Lane, London EC3M 3DX

Herring Son and Daw, 26-28 Sackville Street, London W1X 2QL

Hodgson Impey and Co, 4 King's Arms Yard, London EC2R 7AX

Hongkong and Shanghai Banking Corporation, 99 Bishopsgate, London EC2P 2LA

Inland Revenue, Somerset House, Strand, London WC2R 1LB

Invest in Britain Bureau, Department of Trade and Industry, Kingsgate House, 66-74 Victoria Street, London SW1E 6SJ

Investors in Industry plc, 91 Waterloo Road, London SE1 8XP

Kenneth Leventhal and Co, 2049 Century Park East, Los Angeles, CA 90067, USA

Kenwright and Cox, 38 Chancery Lane, London WC2A 1EZ

Kidsons, Columbia House, 69 Aldwych, London WC2B 4DY

Kleinwort Benson, 20 Fenchurch Street, London EC3P 3DB

KMG Thomson McLintock and Co, 70 Finsbury Pavement, London EC2A 1SX

Lloyds Bank plc, 71 Lombard Street, London EC3P 3BS

Metaport Commodities Ltd, 19-21 Great Tower Street, London EC3R 5AQ

Michael Laurie and Partners, Fitzroy House, 18-20 Grafton Street, London W1X 4DD

Midland Bank Group plc, Poultry, London EC2P 2BX

Moores and Rowland, Clifford's Inn, Fetter Lane, London EC4A 1AS

Morgan Guaranty Trust Co of New York, 1 Angel Court, London EC2R 7AE

Department for National Savings, Charles House, Kensington High Street, London W14 8SD

National Westminster Bank plc, 41 Lothbury, London EC2P 2BP

Neville Russell and Co, 246 Bishopsgate, London EC2M 4PB

Office of Fair Trading, Field House, Bream's Buildings, London EC4A 1PR

Pannell Kerr Forster, New Garden House, 78 Hatton Garden, London EC1 8JA

Peat Marwick Mitchell and Co, Puddle Dock, Blackfriars, London EC4V 3PD

Price Waterhouse and Co, Southwark Towers, 32 London Bridge Street, London SE1 9SY

Richard Ellis and Co, 64 Cornhill, London EC3V 3PS

Risk Management Consultants Ltd, 15 Minories, London EC3N 1NJ

Robson Rhodes and Co, 186 City Road, London EC1V 2NV

Royal Bank of Scotland plc, St Andrew's Square, Edinburgh EH2 2YE

Samuel Montagu Ltd, 114 Old Broad Street, London EC2P 2HY

(Schroders) J Henry Schroder Wagg Ltd, 120 Cheapside, London EC2V 6DS

Spicer and Pegler and Co, Friary Court, 65 Crutched Friars, London EC3N 6DS

Standard Chartered Bank, 10 Clements Lane, London EC4N 7AB

Stewart Wrightson plc, 1 Camomile Street, London EC3A 7HJ

Stock Exchange, Information Department, London EC2N 1HP

Stoy Hayward and Co, 54 Baker Street, London W1M 1DJ

Sun Alliance plc, 1 Bartholomew Lane, London EC2N 2AB

Sun Life of Canada plc, 2-4 Cockspur Street, London SW1Y 5BH

Taiyo Kobe Bank Ltd, P and O Building, Leadenhall Street, London EC3V 4RE

Thomson Local Directories, Thomson House, 296 Farnborough Road, Farnborough, Hampshire GU14 7NU

Touche Ross and Co, Hill House, 1 Little New Street, London EC4A 3TR

Trade Indemnity plc, 12-34 Great Eastern Street, London EC2A 3AX

Department of Trade and Industry, Publicity and Publications Branch, Millbank Tower, Millbank, London SW1P 4QN

HM Treasury, Parliament Street, London SW1P 3AG

Union Bank of Switzerland, 117 Old Broad Street, London EC2N 1AJ

Westpac Banking Corporation plc, Walbrook House, 23 Walbrook, London EC4N 8LD

Index

The Business Guide to Effective Speaking

Making Presentations, Using Audio Visuals, and Dealing with the Media

Jacqueline Dunckel and Elizabeth Parnham

'a practical and concise guide' BRITISH BUSINESS

Effective communication has always been the key to business success and this book provides a straightforward approach to developing techniques to improve on-the-job speaking skills. It is primarily written for businessmen who have to speak in front of colleagues or represent their company in the media. It can also be used as a quick reference source for specific problems. The authors answer most of the problems which affect speakers:

- **How to improve the voice**
- **What to wear on television**
- **How to handle hostile questions**
- **How to chair a meeting.**

£11.95 Hardback *1 85091 056 1*
£5.95 Paperback *1 85091 057 X*
122 pages 216 x 138mm 1985

Promotion for the Professions

A Guide to Practice Development

Ian Linton

'A solid, sensible introduction to practice promotion' WINNING CUSTOMERS

Although recent legislation has lifted advertising bans from accountants, solicitors and other professionals, only a comparatively small number of the professions are allowed to advertise their services. This book considers promotion in its widest sense, covering not only advertising, but also the communication of information (for instance in audio-visual presentations, brochures and leaflets). These techniques of communication are widely used in the professions, even where there are restrictions on advertising.

The practical aspects of the various promotional techniques are discussed in detail, including:

- **How to select the best medium for an advertising campaign**
- **Direct mail**
- **Stages in producing publicity material**
- **Audio-visual presentations**
- **Press relations**
- **Holding presentations and seminars**

'Identifies the various ways in which the professions can grow and prosper in the present tough environment' ACCOUNTANCY AGE

£12.95 Hardback *0 85038 996 8**
134 pages 216 x 138mm 1985

KOGAN PAGE
120 Pentonville Road, London N1 9JN, England